A Cookbook for Men Who Need to Get Out of the Doghouse

Michael Durham

Outskirts Press, Inc.
Denver, Colorado

Outskirts Press
http://www.outskirtspress.com

ISBN-10: 1-59800-025-X
ISBN-13: 978-1-59800-025-2

Outskirts Press and the "OP" logo are trademarks belonging to
Outskirts Press, Inc.

Printed in the United States of America

Dedication

This is dedicated to the one I love.
Oh Yeah, also to Teddy the wonder dog.
And the many times
We spent together in the dog house.
Deaf, smells and a pest,
But still a wonderful dancer.

Table of Contents

Introduction

I am not sure how or where the term started, but all of us guys have made the comment about "being in the dog house".

For me, it started twenty-nine years ago when I asked my new bride what the lumps in her gravy were, and trust me, I have been back as a frequent tenant many times since.

This story makes a lot of sense regarding why the women of the world need a place to send their men.

As a young wife prepared the evening meal, her husband asked why she cut off part of the roast before putting it into the pot. The wife responded that this was how her mother always prepared her roasts. Her own curiosity now piqued, she pondered the question for a time and finally, after being badgered by her inquisitive spouse, curiosity got the best of her and she phoned her mother to find out the reason.

"Mom, I am preparing my roast, and my dear husband asked why I cut off part of it. I told him that was how you always did it and your roast was always great. So why do we cut off part of it?"

The mother replied, "I'm not really sure, but my mother always did, and hers was good, too."

Upon relaying the information once her telephone conversation was over, the young husband, obsessed with the reasoning behind this ritual, asked his wife to call her grandmother to find out why.

She called "Grandma, I am trying to cook a roast, and my husband wants to know why we cut off a piece of it before putting it into the pot. I called Mom, who told me you always did. He asked me to call you directly. Why, Grandma?"

The grandmother replied, "Well dear, my pot was always too small, so I cut some off so it would fit."

The young woman hung up the phone and said, "IT HELPS THE JUICES ESCAPE, and you are in the dog house."

So it began --

Dog House Alerts

I have developed the "Dog House Alert" rating schedule, which is a guide in assisting you in cooking the perfect dish and getting out of the doghouse as soon as possible.

- LOW – The cook has not officially been sent to the doghouse, but receiving the silent treatment means he is not far away.

- LOW to MODERATE – Chances of an overnight visit is elevated, and the cook needs to perform in order to remain free.

- MODERATE – Staying out of the doghouse is getting to be a challenge, but the cook's keen attention to his significant other's needs and the preparation of a great dish will keep him on her good side.

 - MODERATE to HIGH –
Starting to live life in the fast lane, you are trying to decide
between a rhinestone or spiked collar. Proceed with caution
or move over, Rover.

- HIGH – DANGER. You
are in deep trouble and are tired of seeing Rover inside
smiling out at you. Must dazzle her. It doesn't hurt to buy
her something at this stage.

The Code

After years of trying, I have finally deciphered the code. The way back into a woman's heart is to get her out of the kitchen. Yes, dazzle her with your cooking.

It's easy. Just don your best smile and cook with love, while making certain to verbalize that sentiment. You'll notice I've named each dish with something reminiscent of love. Typically, a woman cooks because somewhere back when the gender roles were defined, it was ingrained as something she <u>must</u> do. Interestingly, men cook because:

   a.) we are curious types. I dare one of you to tell me you
        did <u>not</u> disassemble at least one toy as a child, and

   b.) we hate the doghouse.

Before we start, let's review a few of the basics. I have added several important descriptions and/or definitions any would-be cook needs to know.

   Kitchen - The arena where we gladiators are going to
        win our battle and extricate ourselves from the
        doghouse.

   Stove – The source of heat rivaled only by what's in
        store for you once your lovely significant other
        samples your fares.

Refrigerator – Where the beer stays cold.

Sink – The water appliance that could be your ticket back to the doghouse if you do not use it wisely and your lovely wife has to clean up your mess.

Cup – An actual measurement, 8 ounces

Pint – A serving at the pub, but also an actual measurement, 16 ounces or 2 cups.

Quart – A more convenient bottle for beer, but also an actual measurement of 32 ounces, 2 pints or 4 cups.

Tablespoon – The big spoon used for measuring also known as TBSP.

Teaspoon – The little spoon used for measuring also known as tsp.

Pinch – A showing of love when the wife walks by, or as a measurement of less than 1/8 tsp.

Dash – What you will do after you pinch your wife, or as a measurement, less than a pinch.

Combinations - 3 tsp equals 1 TBSP, 2 TBSP equals 1/8 cup, 4 TBSP equals ¼ cup, 8 TBSP equals ½ cup, 12 TBSP equals 3/4 cup and 16 TBSP equals 1 cup.

Spices

The following is a very important part of cooking which could either save or ruin the meal, herbs and spices. (By being overly zealous in my experimentation with seasonings, I once was accused of trying to make my wife sick and ended up in the doghouse). Here are a few that you should know about:

Allspice – I thought it was a combination of everything, but found out it is an actual fruit with a flavor that resembles a blend of cinnamon, cloves and nutmeg.

Basil – The most popular herb in America. The flavor is almost addictive, and there is little upon which a bit of basil can't improve. Known as a tomato's best friend, it is also delicious on chicken, fish, pasta, stew, salads and vegetables. Add basil in the last 10 minutes of cooking, as heat will dissipate its sweet, rich flavor.

Bay Leaves – Actually the dried leafs of a Mediterranean evergreen. It has a sweet, floral aroma and the flavor is perfect for adding to roast pork or chicken, pot roast, turkey, or ham. Use 2-3 leaves and remove before serving. Bay Leaves are also perfect for spaghetti sauce and chicken soup, use 2 per quart. A surprising fact is that Bay Leaves improve the flavor of salt-free dishes with their rich flavor. Note: bay leaves are very light (8 ounces by weight equals one gallon by volume). Remember to remove them when serving the dish, if not, you may be accused of trying to choke her, and back to the doghouse you'll go.

Dill – The predominant flavor in pickles, dill is also used with fish from a seafood boil to herring in cream sauce. It also adds a great flavor to potato salad (The first time I realized I needed glasses was when I added 3 tablespoons of dill instead of 3 teaspoons to a potato salad, I re-named the salad Potato-flavored-dill-salad and you guessed it, back to the dog house).

Mace – Never have used it, but had experience with it back in the 60's and only thought it was a cop thing. I now stand corrected. Mace, the lace-like, dried covering of the nutmeg, is a sweet and flavorful spice well worth using. Mace has a softer flavor than nutmeg, and for a nice change of pace, can be used in place of nutmeg in any recipe. I didn't know, but Mace is a traditional flavoring for doughnuts and hot dogs.

Marjoram – You guessed it, another spice I stayed away from because it just didn't sound right. Marjoram is very popular throughout the Western world and is frequently found in Polish, Italian, Mexican and French cooking. Closely related to oregano, marjoram has a flowery flavor, which is quite strong and flavorful and should be added near the end of cooking. Marjoram improves the flavor of tomato sauce, bean soup, marinated vegetables and salad dressing.

Oregano – We all know this one, for Italian spaghetti sauces to Greek salads to Turkish kebobs, the sweet, strong flavor of Mediterranean oregano is perfect. Oregano should be added in the beginning of cooking, so the flavor has time to come out and blend with the other flavors of the dish. Add while browning onions or beef for both spaghetti sauce and chili. It's also great for any tomato dish or Italian specialty (Little known fact, Oregano is also from the mint family).

Paprika – I have only used it for making a chicken or turkey look appetizing. It is actually a sweet red pepper, great for not only adding color, but also a rich pleasing flavor.

Rosemary – Ahh Rosemary, brings back some memories, oops not too loud or it's the doghouse again. An herb resembling a curved pine needle, the savory, almost minty sweetness of rosemary makes it perfect for pork and lamb, from grilled chops to large roasts. Rosemary adds a great flavor to almost everything like chicken and fish. You have to try it in mashed potatoes.

Sage – One of the richest and most distinctive flavors of all the herbs. Perfect for baked chicken or pork, sprinkle with lemon juice or salt, sage and pepper. Sage is traditionally used for poultry stuffing and breakfast sausages, but its rich strength lends itself well to many dishes, such as beef roasts, pork chops and game dishes like venison, duck and goose. Sage has become much more popular in recent years. Try adding it to flavor salt-free dishes, sprinkling on turkey breasts or adding to soups and sauces.

Thyme - Thyme is one of the best cooking herbs in the world and has a strong and distinctive flavor that goes great with poultry and pork. With garlic and pepper, rub on chicken or fish for the grill, or mix with rosemary, garlic and pepper for a great roast or fish fry.

I hope these few tidbits will assist you in your quest and by the way -- start looking for a dog, 'cause there is going to be plenty of room in the dog house now that you are cooking with love."

The Warm-Up

Lovebuie
(Okay to call it Buckbuie during deer season)

DOGHOUSE ALERT:

LOW to MODERATE

This little number may even gain you some brownie points with the old gal (oops scratch that, use "the most wonderful woman in the world"). If not, this recipe will help time pass while in the doghouse.

Ingredients:

    Pure maple syrup
    Scotch whiskey
    Anisette

Prep:

    3 parts maple syrup to one part scotch and slowly add anisette to taste and mix well.

Moderation in all things.
- Terence -

APPETIZERS

Seafood Dip for the Most Beautiful Woman in the World

DOGHOUSE ALERT:

LOW

Warning! Be prepared or alert level may rise. You must have the correct response for, "Oh what, you think I'm fat?" when she sees you are using light cream cheese.

Ingredients:

- 1 – 8 oz. can of shrimp
- 1 – 8 oz. can of crabmeat
- 8 oz. light cream cheese (No, Love of My Life, you do not look fat and certainly don't warrant light ingredients, I just prefer a light dip.)
- 8 oz. mayonnaise – If you are watching fat, try reduced calorie, but not fat-free
- ¼ cup chopped onion
- ¼ cup chopped celery
- 1 – Love gaze

Prep:

Mix ingredients together and serve on crackers or chips.

One word frees us of all the weight and pain of life:
That word is love. – Sophocles

Artichoke Dip for Your Hottie

DOGHOUSE ALERT:

LOW

Make sure the artichokes are cut to a size she enjoys; you don't want to choke her.

Ingredients:

2 – 14 oz. cans of artichokes
1 cup of mayonnaise – If you are watching fat, try
   reduced calorie, but not fat-free
1 cup of grated parmesan cheese
8 oz. grated part-skim mozzarella cheese
Garlic powder to taste
1 – "Wow, you look great"

Prep:

Drain artichokes and chop. Mix all ingredients in an ovenproof dish and bake at 350 degrees for 20 to 25 minutes. Serve with crackers or chips.

Death is not the worst that can happen to men.
- Plato -

Princess's Salmon Dip

DOGHOUSE ALERT:

MODERATE to HIGH

You are teetering on the edge, looks like no way out, but a Salmon dip could be just the ticket to redeem yourself. Again, you must have the correct response for using light cream cheese and not too much horseradish, nothing more unattractive than a woman with her face red and steam coming out her ears.

Ingredients:

    8 oz. of light cream cheese (No, Love of My Life, you
        are not fat.)
    2 tsp chopped green onion
    2 tsp ketchup
    1 tsp horseradish
    8 oz. salmon, flaked
    1 – Over do it (tell her the Salmon is from Alaska)

Prep:

Blend all ingredients until well mixed.   Serve with crackers or vegetables.

To be loved, be lovable.
- Ovid -

Hommous for the Queen

MODERATE

Not too much garlic or she will blame you for the garlic breath.

Ingredients:

  1 – 16 oz. can of chickpeas
  ½ cup of Sesame Tahini – Mix this well
  1 TBSP of minced garlic (save a step and buy this in jars
      pre-minced)
  Juice of 2 or 3 lemons per taste
  Salt and pepper to taste
  1 – "Your hair looks great."

Prep:

In saucepan bring chickpeas to a boil for 1 minute. Pour into food processor, add Tahini, garlic and blend adding lemon, salt and pepper to taste. Serve warm or cold with Pita bread triangles, radishes or celery stalks.

Every man is guilty of all the good he didn't do.
- Voltaire -

Anchovy Mushrooms
(Because your wife is oh so sweet)

DOGHOUSE ALERT:

LOW

You are in her good graces, but remember the tides do turn. Just hope she likes anchovies, if not be prepared to tell her that you thought she might try something daring being such a contemporary woman and you appreciate that in her.

Ingredients:

6 small white mushrooms
2 TBSP breadcrumbs
2 TBSP Parmesan cheese
2 tps extra-virgin olive oil
1 tps parsley
1 tps red wine vinegar
1 anchovy flat fillet (pasted)

Prep:

Preheat oven to 350 degrees. Remove mushroom stems, mince and stir in bread crumbs, Parmesan, olive oil, parsley, vinegar, anchovy paste (mash anchovy fillet with 2 forks until it forms a paste). Add salt and pepper to taste. Stir mixture until it is combined well. Arrange the mushroom caps on a baking sheet and fill the cavities with approximately 1 tsp of stuffing (ok to mound). Place baking sheet on the middle rack and bake for 15 mins. Sprinkle caps slightly with parsley and serve.

There is always some madness in love.
But there is also always some reason in madness.
- Friedrich Nietzsche -

Parmesan Canapés for Your Goddess

DOGHOUSE ALERT:

MODERATE

You chance being accused of trying to fatten her up with the bread. Tell her it isn't so, just look at the name, you named it after her and not Junior's young teacher.

Ingredients:

12 slices of bread, crusts removed and cut into triangles
1 cup lump crabmeat
2/3 cup mayonnaise
2/3 cup Parmesan cheese
4 finely chopped scallions
1 tps lemon juice
1 - Apology for the Junior's young teacher comment

Prep:

Preheat oven to 400 degrees. Toast bread on baking sheet in oven until golden brown. In a bowl, mix crab, mayonnaise, Parmesan, scallions and lemon juice. Add salt and pepper to taste. Reduce oven to 375 degrees. Spread crab mixture on toasts and bake on middle rack for 10 minutes.

There is no remedy for love but to love more.
- Henry David Thoreau -

Seasoned Oil of Love

DOGHOUSE ALERT:

LOW

Do not get over confident with yourself. Remember you are only one comment away from the doghouse at all times.

Ingredients:

¼ tsp oregano
¼ tsp basil
¼ tsp rosemary
¼ tsp kosher salt
2 pinches black pepper
pinch red pepper
extra-virgin olive oil
Sourdough or warmed bread of your choosing
1 – Let's just cuddle tonight

Prep:

In a low bowl or lipped plate add dry ingredients. Slowly add the olive oil 1 TBSP at a time until the Oil of Love is at desired mix. Dip warm sourdough bread or rolls that have been warmed slightly and enjoy.

Once a word has been allowed to escape,
it cannot be recalled.
- Horace -

Sausage Roll for Your Love

DOGHOUSE ALERT:

MODERATE to HIGH

A great way out of the doghouse, but the bread issue again. Be ready to tell her she is looking way too thin, although still as beautiful as ever.

Ingredients:

> 1 ½ lb. hot sausage (loose)
> 8 oz. shredded mozzarella
> 1 bag pizza dough (find this in the refrigerated section of your grocery store)
> 2 eggs

Prep:

Fry and drain sausage and let cool. Mix cooled sausage, eggs and mozzarella. Spread dough on a cookie sheet and cover with the sausage mixture. Roll into a loaf. Brush oil on sides of a loaf pan and place loaf into it. Let loaf rise for 1 hour and then bake at 425 degrees for 15 mins. Then lower oven to 375 degrees and continue baking for 35 minutes.

A companion's words of persuasion are effective.
- Homer -

24

Light Cream Cheese Ball
(No you are not fat)

DOGHOUSE ALERT:

LOW

The light cream cheese once again, you must know the response by now, if not, expect the heightened alert status.

Ingredients:

11 oz. softened light cream cheese
1 TBSP minced onion
1 TBSP finely chopped dill pickle
1 TBSP chopped pepperoni
1 TBSP Romano cheese
½ tsp. Garlic salt
1 TBSP pickle juice
Chopped nuts
1 "Wow, what a woman"

Prep:

Combine all ingredients, except nuts, in a bowl and mix well. Roll into a ball and refrigerate for 2 hours. Cover ball with chopped nuts and serve with crackers.

I pay very little regard...to what any young person
says on the subject of marriage. If they profess
a disinclination for it,
I only set it down that they have not yet
seen the right person.
– Jane Austen –

SOUPS

Bisque Amour

DOGHOUSE ALERT:

HIGH

No possible way to mess up with this one, an excellent dish and excellent way to be back indoors once again. You could even get away with telling her she looks a little chubby (however, from personal experience, I really don't recommend your saying that).

Ingredients:

1 stick of butter
½ cup diced onion
2 tsp of minced garlic
½ cup diced celery
1 cup of crushed tomatoes
½ cup of flour
¼ cup cognac
1 cup of white wine
1 quart and 2 cups of skim milk
1 lb of seafood (use whatever you like such as lobster, shrimp, scallops or a combination like scallops, shrimp, lump crabmeat, clams, diced fish)
1 tsp lemon juice
1 tsp. Paprika
2 TBSP chopped basil
salt and pepper to taste
Cayenne pepper to taste (go easy with it)

Prep:

Melt the butter and sauté the onions, garlic, celery and tomatoes for +/- 10 minutes. Stir in flour until the mixture is smooth. Slowly add the cognac, white wine and milk stirring constantly bringing it to a slow boil. Add all seafood, lemon juice and paprika and bring back to a slow boil. Simmer for 30 minutes then add basil, salt, pepper and cayenne pepper.

It is a great thing to know our vices.
– Cicero –

Mary P's Chowder of Love

DOGHOUSE ALERT:

LOW to MODERATE

Make sure the clams are shell-free and your life will remain hell-free.

Ingredients:

2 lbs. mixed sea food
1/2 pint minced clams
1 tsp Seafood Seasoning
Salt to taste
½ tsp black pepper
1 ½ cups minced onion
3 cups potatoes, chopped
1 cup celery
¼ lb. bacon in fine bits
¼ cup parsley
½ oz. Brandy
½ oz. cream sherry.
Milk
Butter
Paprika
1 – "I love the way your eyes sparkle"

Prep:

Place all fish in a large pan and cover with cold water. Add 1 tps. Seafood Seasoning, (salt, if desired) and ½ tsp black pepper. Bring to a boil and simmer until tender (15 to 20 minutes). Cool. Break up seafood into bite size pieces, being careful to remove any bones, skin or fatty pieces.

While seafood is cooking in a large frying pan sauté the minced onions, potatoes, celery and bacon.

Add to pan with seafood and simmer until potatoes are tender. Add parsley, brandy and cream sherry.

Chowder base is now ready for use or freezing. Use equal parts of chowder base and milk adding a little cream if you want a richer sauce. Serve with butter and paprika.

Happiness depends upon ourselves.
– Aristotle –

Cream of It-Doesn't-Matter
It's From the Heart

DOGHOUSE ALERT:

MODERATE to HIGH

It is best not to tell her about the butter, and keep the wine handy, pour her a glass to loosen her up.

Ingredients:

1 stick of butter
½ cup diced onion
2 tsp of minced garlic
½ cup diced celery
½ cup of flour
1 cup of white wine
1 quart and 2 cups of skim milk
1 lb of fresh vegetable (broccoli or cauliflower or mushrooms or artichoke hearts or asparagus or a combination of all, it's your creation, but choose wisely or it is back to the doghouse.)
1 tsp. paprika
2 TBSP chopped basil
salt and pepper to taste

Prep:

Melt the butter and sauté the onions, garlic and celery for +/- 10 minutes. Stir in flour until the mixture is smooth. Slowly add the white wine and milk stirring constantly bringing it to a slow boil. Add the vegetable and paprika and bring back to a slow boil. Simmer for 30 minutes then add basil, salt, pepper.

There is a demand in these days for men
who can make wrong appear right.
– Terence –

Split Pea Soup for Lovers

DOGHOUSE ALERT:

MODERATE

Taste before serving, you want it seasoned to perfection because she is perfection (and tell her that), but a bland pea soup will appear as if you do not care and are only with her for one reason.

Ingredients:

½ gallon of water
1 ham bone (with some meat)
1 lb. dry split peas
1 cup of chopped onion
1 carrot chopped
1 clove of garlic
2 tsp salt
¼ tsp thyme
1 bay leaf
1 tsp sugar
¼ tsp marjoram
¼ tsp ground black pepper
Lemon juice to taste
Worcestershire sauce to taste
Dash of second reason you are with her

Prep:

Put all ingredients in large pot and simmer, partially covered, for 3 hours stirring occasionally. Remove bay leaf and ham bone. Cut meat off bone and return the meat to pot. If a thinner soup is desired, add milk accordingly. If more meat is required, add cubed ham.

The cause is hidden. The effect is visible to all.
– Ovid –

Baby Doll Lamb Shank Soup

DOGHOUSE ALERT:

HIGH

No worries, you will be back among the human race soon unless you misbehave while it's cooking.

Ingredients:

Lamb shank with meat (left over from Baby Doll
    Roasted Leg of Lamb page 57)
1 cup of chopped celery with leaves
1 small diced onion
1 tsp of minced garlic
1 tsp of allspice
salt and pepper to taste
2 TBPS Beef base
1 - 16 oz can of Veg-all
1 - 16 oz can of Italian seasoned diced tomatoes
A pinch of baking soda
1- 8 oz jar of sliced mushrooms
3 Bay leaves
1 cup of dry egg noodles
5 minutes of the "love dance"

Prep:

Place shank in a stock pot, cover with water and boil for 1 minute, then empty water. Return to heat with no water and sear shank until a little stock is formed. Cover shank with water again and add onion, celery, garlic, bay leaves, allspice and beef base and let simmer partially covered for 4 hours. Add tomatoes and continue simmering for 1 hour. Add the baking soda, noodles and continue simmering for 10 minutes. Add Veg-all, mushrooms, season to taste, remove bay leaves and serve.

O tyrant love,
to what do you not drive the hearts of men.
– Virgil –

Chicken Soup
(To keep your baby strong and healthy)

DOGHOUSE ALERT:

MODERATE

Make sure you season it properly or you may properly spend the next season in the house of dog.

Ingredients:

1 skinless and boneless chicken breast (1 inch cubes)
1 skinless and boneless chicken thigh (1 inch cubes)
2 celery stalks (1 inch pieces)
2 carrots (coin cut into ¼ inch pieces)
1 – medium onion (cut into ½ inch pieces)
2 TBSP minced fresh parsley
1 clove minced garlic
6 chicken bouillon cubes
½ tsp black pepper
1 bay leaf
6 cups water

Prep:

In a large saucepan add all ingredients and cook on low heat, covered for 1 hour, stirring occasionally.

Any thing too stupid to be said is sung.
– Voltaire –

SALADS

Caesar Salad for Your Precious

DOGHOUSE ALERT:

MODERATE to HIGH

Just follow directions and she will be yours, however, make sure your anchovy paste is just that. No chunks.

Ingredients:

1 tsp minced garlic
4 anchovy fillets (flat)
1 tsp salt
Juice from ½ lemon
1 tsp black pepper
1 tsp Worcestershire sauce
½ tsp Dijon mustard
1 TBSP mayonnaise
1/3 cup of extra-virgin olive oil
2 heads of Romaine lettuce
¼ - ½ cup grated Romano cheese
¼ - ½ cup grated Parmesan cheese
1 – Wink

Prep:

Place salt, garlic and anchovies in a large salad bowl and mash into a paste. Whisk in lemon juice, pepper, Worcestershire sauce, mustard and mayonnaise. Whisk in olive oil. Wash, dry and chop Romaine into 1½ inch pieces and add to the bowl. Add ½ cup of seasoned croutons and cheese. Toss mixture well and serve.

To lengthen thy life, lessen thy meals.
– Benjamin Franklin –

Brutus Salad for the Love of Your Life
(Why Brutus? It is a Caesar salad betrayed)

DOGHOUSE ALERT:

MODERATE

Make sure she likes scallops in her salad, but you should already know that.

Ingredients:

1 tsp minced garlic
4 anchovy fillets (flat)
1 tsp salt
Juice from ½ lemon
1 tsp black pepper
1 tsp Worcestershire sauce
½ tsp Dijon mustard
1 TBSP mayonnaise
1/3 cup of extra-virgin olive oil
2 heads of Romaine lettuce
½ cup grated Romano cheese
½ cup grated Parmesan cheese
1 lb Sea Scallops or Shrimp or combination of both
¼ cup of Seasoned Oil of Love (see below)

Prep:

Place salt, garlic and anchovies in a large salad bowl and mash into a paste. Whisk in lemon juice, pepper, Worcestershire sauce, mustard and mayonnaise. Whisk in olive oil. Wash, dry and chop Romaine into 1½ inch pieces and add to the bowl. Add ½ cup of seasoned croutons and cheese. Toss mixture well. Wash Scallops and coat evenly with Seasoned Oil of Love. Broil on high until done, turning as required. Add to salad and serve.

Seasoned Oil of Love: SEE PAGE 22

Prep:

In a low bowl or lipped plate add dry ingredients. Slowly add the olive oil 1 TBSP at a time until the Oil of Love is at desired mix.

It is better, of course,
to know useless things than to know nothing.
— Seneca —

Spinach Salad for Life's Little Specialty

DOGHOUSE ALERT:

LOW

Should not be any reasons for her to complain, but throw in a few "I appreciate yous".

Ingredients:

2 packages of fresh spinach
4 hard-boiled eggs
4 slices of cooked bacon cut into ¼ inch pieces
½ pound fresh mushrooms, sliced
Dressing:
¼ cup finely chopped onion
¼ cup sweet pickle relish
3 TBSP parsley
2 TBSP pimento
1 hard-boiled egg, chopped
1 cup extra virgin olive oil
1/3 cup vinegar
1 ½ tsp sugar
1 ½ tsp salt
Garlic powder to taste

Prep:

Wash spinach and tear into bite size pieces and place in a bowl. Layer sliced mushrooms on top of spinach. Slice the hard-boiled eggs and arrange over mushrooms. Sprinkle bacon bits over salad.

Dressing: Mix all ingredients together and shake well. Pour over salad and toss.

By all means marry;
if you get a good wife, you'll be happy.
If you get a bad one,
you'll become a philosopher.
— Socrates —

Tabouli From the Heart

DOGHOUSE ALERT:

MODERATE

Do not over-do it with the cracked wheat; this is a salad not a wheat fest.

Ingredients:

6 scant handfuls of #1 size cracked wheat (bulgur wheat)
6 bunches of fresh Italian flat leafed parsley
3 bunches of scallions
6 tomatoes
Juice of 4 to 6 lemons to taste
¼ cup of chopped mint leaves
½ cup of extra virgin olive oil or until salad glistens
½ tsp of allspice
salt and pepper to taste
1 – "This salad's freshness reminds me of the freshness of your being"

Prep:

In a large bowl, place cracked wheat. Chop parsley very fine and add to bowl. Chop scallions into 1/8 inch pieces and add to bowl. Chop tomatoes into ¼ inch pieces and add to bowl. Add lemon juice, mint, and allspice and toss salad until mixed well. Slowly add olive oil while continuously tossing and stop once the entire salad glistens. Add salt and pepper to taste.

He who is in love is wise and becoming wiser,
sees newly every time he looks at the object beloved,
drawing from it with his eyes and his mind
those virtues which it possesses.
– Ralph Waldo Emerson –

Potato Salad for Your Petite

DOGHOUSE ALERT:

LOW

I've never seen a bad potato salad. If she says she cannot eat it because she is too fat your automatic response is, "NOOOOO you are not too fat! I'm the fat one"

Ingredients:

5 large potatoes
8 hard-boiled eggs
1 medium onion
8 oz. jar of chopped pimento
¾ cup mayonnaise
½ cup Dijon mustard
2 TBSP parsley
Salt and Pepper to taste
Paprika
1 – I love you

Prep:

Cook unpeeled potatoes until skins are tender. Peel potatoes (if desired) and cut into small cubes. Dice eggs and onions and add to potatoes. Combine mayonnaise, parsley, salt and pepper (to taste) and garnish with paprika.

When you fish for love,
bait with your heart, not your brain.
— Mark Twain —

Your Darling's Cole Slaw

DOGHOUSE ALERT:

LOW

Some people only like cole slaw on their BBQ sandwich, proceed with caution.

Ingredients:

6 cups chopped cabbage
½ cup chopped green pepper
1 medium onion, chopped
8 oz. jar of pimentos, chopped
1 – Love stare

Marinade Dressing:

½ cup vegetable oil
1/3 cup sugar
¼ tsp salt
½ cup wine vinegar
½ cup water

Prep:

Place salad ingredients in a large bowl and toss well. Mix marinade ingredients, shake well in a jar and pour over slaw. Toss lightly, cover and refrigerate the day before serving. Toss several times during the marinating period.

Variation: For a creamy dressing

    4 cups mayonnaise
    ¼ cup vinegar
    ½ cup sugar
    1 TBSP mustard
    Add milk to thin as needed.

Prep:

    Mix well and store in refrigerator.

It is with our passions, as it is with fire and water;
they are good servants but bad masters.
— Aesop —

MAIN DISHES

Baby Doll Roasted Leg of Lamb

DOGHOUSE ALERT:

HIGH

It is a winner, just don't call it mutton and the doghouse will contain nuttin'.

Ingredients:

    1 Leg of Lamb
    Garlic cloves
    Rosemary
    Salt and pepper
    1- Gaze of adoration

Prep:

Make ½ inch slits all over the leg of lamb. Slice garlic cloves lengthwise and insert one half into each slit. Cover leg generously with fresh Rosemary. Add ½ tsp each of salt and pepper to the leg. Bake at 350 degrees until done to your desired state (rare = 140 degrees, medium = 150 degrees, well-done = 160 degrees).

He only employs his passion
who can make no use of his reason.
– Cicero –

Perfect Grilled Chicken
(Perfect, just like your wife)

DOGHOUSE ALERT:

LOW

Do not undercook the chicken and make sure all the feathers are removed.

Ingredients:

Skinless, boneless chicken breasts (1 per person)
Italian dressing – Her favorite bottled brand

Prep:

Fold individual breasts in wax paper and pound to ¼ inch with kitchen mallet. Place all breasts in a shallow bowl or pan and cover with the Italian dressing. Cover and refrigerate for 2 hours. Fire up the grill, discard dressing and cook breasts until done.

Waste no more time talking about great souls
and how they should be.
Become one yourself!
– Marcus Aurelius Antoninus –

Mustard Salmon Honey

DOGHOUSE ALERT:

MODERATE

A great honey-mustard flavor, just follow the directions and maybe later you can muster up some honey.

Ingredients:

    2 8oz salmon fillets
    3 TBSP Dijon mustard
    1 TBSP honey
    2 TBSP breadcrumbs
    1 tsp softened butter
    1 TBSP chopped parsley
    salt
    pepper
    1 – Song of seduction

Prep:

Preheat oven to 400 degrees. Mix honey and mustard and spread over the salmon. Mix butter, parsley and bread crumbs and top the fillets. Bake for 10 to 15 minutes. Add salt and pepper to taste.

I am not sincere, even when I say I am not.
– Jules Renard –

Salmon Swimming From the Gates of Hell
(Over Couscous with Love)

DOGHOUSE ALERT:

HIGH

Some people don't like their salmon messed with, but I say mess with it.

Ingredients:

2 TBSP extra-virgin olive oil
1 tsp minced garlic
16 oz artichoke hearts
8 oz jar of pink vodka sauce
4 - cherry peppers – diced
12 Calamata olives
1 cup uncooked couscous
12 oz salmon
Parmesan cheese

Prep:

Brown the garlic in olive oil over medium high heat and add artichokes, cherry peppers and olives. Continue cooking over medium heat for 10 minutes. Cut salmon into 1½ inch cubes and add to mixture along with the vodka sauce. Continue cooking until couscous is ready.

Prepare couscous per instructions.

In a bowl or deep-dish plate, place a bed of couscous and add salmon mixture. Add Parmesan cheese and serve.

Variations:

<u>Salmon and Friends Swimming From the Gates of Hell</u>

Reduce salmon to 6 oz and add 6 oz of shrimp or scallops or crab or mild fish or any combination of these. Add Fava beans to mixture. Serve over pasta.

He, who comes first, eats first.
– Eike von Repkow ---

Roast Chicken for Your Perfect

DOGHOUSE ALERT:

LOW

No one can mess up a roasted chicken. If you do then maybe you do belong in the doghouse.

Ingredients:

1 whole chicken
1 tsp salt
½ tsp black pepper
paprika
1 – Tarzan yell (women flip for this)

Prep:

Preheat oven to 325 degrees. Rub the chicken inside and out with the salt and pepper and dust breast with paprika. Place chicken on an oiled rack set into a roasting pan and roast about 1 hour or when a thermometer inserted into the thickest part of the thigh reads 165 degrees.

Variations:

Lemon Pepper Chicken – Cut a fresh lemon in half and insert into the chicken cavity and increase pepper to 1 tsp. Cook until done.

Garlic Chicken – Place 1 TBSP minced garlic into the chicken cavity and cook until done.

Lemon Peppered Garlic Chicken – Cut a fresh lemon in half and insert into the chicken cavity and increase pepper to 1 tsp and Place 1 TBSP minced garlic into the chicken cavity…hey what the heck add 1 whole Bay leaf as well.

Preach not to others what they should eat,
but eat as becomes you, and be silent.
– Epictetus –

Lamb Chops Filled With Love
(On The Grill)

DOGHOUSE ALERT:

LOW to MODERATE

Proceed with caution, not everyone likes the cheese, so prepare a few without the Stilton and redeem yourself.

Ingredients:

Lamb chops
Bleu Cheese (I prefer Stilton)
Salt and pepper

Prep:

Fire up the grill. Rub chops with salt and pepper to taste. Butterfly (cut) the chops and insert a slice of bleu cheese. Grill for 5 minutes a side or until done to your wonderful lady's satisfaction.

Part of the secret of success in life is to eat what you like
and let the food fight it out inside.
– Mark Twain –

Grilled Trout
(Because they are the rainbows of our lives)

DOGHOUSE ALERT:

MODERATE

You can't mess up a trout, just don't burn it and remember the reason you like rainbow trout is because she is the rainbow in your life.

Ingredients:

Fresh, cleaned trout
Lemon slices
Butter
Salt and pepper
1 – Compliment on her shoes

Prep:

Fire up the grill. Rub fish with salt and pepper and place on a sheet of aluminum foil. Place 2 or 3 lemon slices (depends on size of fish) on top of fish. Place 2 or 3¼ inch slices of butter on fish. Fold foil tightly around fish and place on grill. Cook for approximately 5 to 10 minutes per side depending on size of fish and heat of the grill. Special care should be given not to overcook. Remove fish from foil and place on platter, use lemon slices as garnish.

Man is what he eats.
– Ludwig Feuerbach –

Angel's Meat Loaf

DOGHOUSE ALERT:

LOW

Don't ruin this by being a lazy cook. Garnish with some fresh parsley sprigs.

Ingredients:

1 lb. Ground sirloin
1 stalk of celery chopped
1 small onion diced
½ green bell pepper diced
2 eggs
1 cup of seasoned bread crumbs
1 Tsp Worcestershire sauce
¼ tsp pepper
½ tsp salt
1 tsp of minced garlic
½ cup ketchup
½ cup of maple syrup

Prep:

Mix all ingredients together except ketchup and maple syrup and place in a loaf pan. Create a ½ inch lengthwise well in top of meat loaf. Mix together ketchup and maple syrup and pour over meatloaf. Bake at 375 degrees for 45 minutes, or until done.

If hunger makes you irritable,
better eat and be pleasant.
– Sefer Hasidium –

SIDES

Rolls of Harmony

DOGHOUSE ALERT:

MODERATE

Yeast rolls can be tricky, but as with your wife, have patience.

Ingredients:

2 cups milk
4 TBSP butter
2 tsp salt
2 TBSP sugar
1 package dry yeast
white flour
melted butter
1 – "Let's go shopping"

Prep:

Heat milk until warm and add to a large bowl. Mix in the butter, sugar and salt. Cool to lukewarm.

Mix the yeast with 1/4 cup warm water and let stand for 5 minutes until dissolved.

Add 3 cups of flour and the dissolved yeast to the milk mixture and beat for 2 minutes. Cover and let dough rise in a warm place until it doubles in size.

Stir the dough well and add as much flour as necessary to knead the dough (2 to 3 cups). Place dough onto a floured surface and knead for two minutes. Allow the dough to sit for 10 minutes. Continue kneading until the mixture is smooth. On a buttered cookie sheet place shaped rolls close together, brush them with melted butter (make sure butter gets between rolls). Cover the rolls and let them rise until they double in size. Bake in a pre-heated oven at 425 for 12 to 15 minutes. During the last few minutes of baking, you can brush lightly with melted butter and add ground Rosemary or Basil to add that special herb taste to the batch. However, these are winners by themselves.

Love is composed of a single soul inhabiting two bodies
— Aristotle —

Perfect Baked Potato for the Perfect Woman

DOGHOUSE ALERT – N/A

It's perfect just like her.

Ingredients:

Russet potatoes
Extra-virgin olive oil
Kosher salt

Prep:

Preheat oven to 350 degrees. Wash and dry the potatoes and poke several holes in them with a fork. Coat lightly with the oil and sprinkle with the salt. Place directly onto the oven rack and cook until done +/- 1 hour depending on the number of potatoes. Also, to avoid going back to the doghouse, place a cookie sheet below the potatoes to catch any oil that may drip.

But love is blind and loves cannot see.
The pretty follies that themselves commit;
For if they could,
Cupid himself would blush
To see me thus transformed to a boy
― William Shakespeare ―

Rosemary Potatoes for Your Sweet

DOGHOUSE ALERT:

LOW

Just make sure the potatoes are done.

Ingredients:

Red potatoes
Extra-virgin olive oil
Rosemary

Prep:

Preheat oven to 350 degrees. Wash, dry and cut potatoes in to 1 ½ inch pieces and coat with oil. Place into a cookie sheet and sprinkle potatoes with rosemary and bake until the potatoes are golden brown, turning as required.

The only man who is really free is the one who can turn down an invitation to dinner without giving an excuse.
– Jules Renard –

Rosemary Mashed Potatoes
(For Ms. Sweet Thing)

DOGHOUSE ALERT:

LOW

The ricer takes out all of the lumps, no problems with this baby.

Ingredients:

1 ½ potatoes per serving
1 TSP butter per serving
1 TSP sour cream per serving
1 tsp fresh ground Rosemary
Salt
Pepper

Prep:

Peel potatoes and boil until soft. With a potato ricer mash potatoes into a large bowl. (If you do not have a potato ricer, mash the best you can.) Stir in butter, sour cream, and rosemary blending it well. Add salt and pepper to taste.

When love is not madness, it is not love
— Pedro Calderon de la Barca —

Fried Potatoes with Green Peppers and Onions
(to add a little excitement)

DOGHOUSE ALERT:

LOW

It's an easy one, but make a fuss so she thinks you are slaving over the dish for her.

Ingredients:

6 potatoes
1 Bell pepper
½ onion
Extra virgin olive oil
Salt
Pepper
1 – Neck rub

Prep:

Over medium heat cover bottom of a pan with extra virgin olive oil. Wash potatoes, bell pepper and onion and cut into ¼ inch slices and add to pan. Cover and cook until potatoes are soft. Salt and pepper to taste.

There are people who strictly deprive themselves
of each and every eatable, drinkable and smokable
which has in any way acquired a shady reputation.
They pay this price for health.
And health is all they get for it.
How strange it is. It is like paying out your
whole fortune for a cow that has gone dry.
— Mark Twain —

Warm You Up Garlic Broccoli

DOGHOUSE ALERT:

LOW

Easy one, perfect for warming her up.

Ingredients:

2 heads broccoli
4 TSP butter
2 rounded TSP minced garlic
Salt
Pepper
Extra virgin olive oil

Prep:

In a saucepan boil broccoli until soft (overcook) and drain. While broccoli is draining return pan to stove and cover the bottom with extra virgin olive oil and add butter and garlic (do not burn garlic). Return the broccoli to the pan and cook for 5 minutes mixing all ingredients well. Add salt and pepper to taste.

The discovery of a new dish does more
for human happiness than the discovery of a new star.
– Anthelme Brillat-Savarin –

Sassy Grilled Vegetables
(Yes my love, because you are sassy)

DOGHOUSE ALERT – N/A

Just don't be too sassy or it might backfire on you.

Ingredients:

1 bunch asparagus
3 small zucchini
3 small yellow squash
salt & pepper to taste
extra virgin olive oil

Prep:

Fire up the grill.

Wash vegetables and cut zucchini and squash into ¼ inch slices or ¼ inch lengthwise pieces. Hold the asparagus at each end and bend until it breaks in two. Discard the stock end and use the flowered end only. In a large bowl add all vegetables and add enough olive oil to make them glisten and add salt and pepper to taste. Wrap all vegetables in aluminum foil and place on grill over low heat. Cook for about 10 minutes or until they are at the consistency you want, be careful not to overcook. Remove and serve.

For a variation add your favorite spices to the mixture

and/or place vegetables without the foil directly onto the grill turning frequently.

Happiness: a good bank account,
a good cook and a good digestion.
– Jean Jacques Rousseau –

DESSERTS

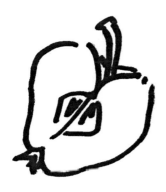

Love Torte

DOGHOUSE ALERT:

MODERATE

Follow the directions and you cannot miss. Not a real sweet dessert, so she will think you are watching out for her sugar intake, just agree with her.

Ingredients:

1 stick of softened butter
¾ cup plus 1 TBSP sugar
1 cup sifted flour
1 tsp baking soda
2 eggs
1/8 tsp salt
12 purple plums
1 tsp cinnamon
1 – Love pat

Prep:

Preheat oven to 350 degrees. Mix the sugar and softened butter until its consistency is creamy. Add the eggs, baking powder, flour and salt and beat until mixed very well. Place into a 9-inch spring form pan (un-greased). Cut the plums into halves and cover the top skin side down. Mix the cinnamon with 1 TSP of sugar and sprinkle over the top. Arrange the oven rack in the lower third of the oven and bake for 45 minutes. Torte is done when a cake tester is inserted and comes out clean. Remove from oven and serve with ice cream or not or let cool. Can be reheated, refrigerated or frozen.

Though this be madness, yet there is method in it.
– William Shakespeare –

Apple of Your Eye Pie

DOGHOUSE ALERT:

HIGH

Be ready. If the crust is too flaky – it's "because I thought you loved a flaky crust." If the crust is not flaky enough – it's "because I thought you hated a flaky crust." If the pie is too tart – it's "because I thought you loved a tart pie." If the pie is not tart enough – it's "because I thought you hated a tart pie." Any other complaints just go back to the doghouse.

Crust (another option is to buy a couple of 9 or 10 inch ready made pie crusts)

Ingredients:

2 cups of flour
1 TBSP of sugar
¼ tsp salt
1 stick butter
1/3 cup of vegetable shortening
TBSP cold water
1 – Wolf whistle

Prep:

In a large mixing bowl sift in sugar, salt and flour, cut butter into pieces and add to bowl, add shortening and mix

85

until you have small pea sized shapes. Slowly add the cold water to mixture and knead until dough starts coming together (be careful not to over mix). Place dough in refrigerator wrapped in plastic wrap for 45 to 60 minutes before rolling out crusts. When ready lightly flour your rolling pin and surface and roll 2 crusts to fit the pie pan.

Apple mixture

Ingredients:

2 pounds of Granny Smith's apples
½ cup sugar
½ cup brown sugar
2 TBSP lemon juice
2 TBSP flour
1 tsp cinnamon
¼ tsp nutmeg
¼ tsp salt
2 TBSP cold butter
Milk for brushing the crusts

Prep:

Pre-heat oven to 375 degrees. Peel, core and slice apples into eighths and add to a large bowl. Add sugar, brown sugar, cinnamon, nutmeg, flour, salt and lemon juice. Mix by tossing ingredients until combined well. Spoon apple mixture into pie shells, dot with cold butter pieces and cover with top crust. Brush a light coating of milk over the top crust and sprinkle with 2 TSP of sugar. Place into oven and bake for 45 to 60 minutes. Remove and enjoy.

Thou shouldst eat to live; not live to eat.
– Socrates –

Aunt Mary Dugan's Sponge Cake

DOGHOUSE ALERT:

LOW

Simple little recipe that will bring back memories of your Aunt Mary, only caution is if your wife thinks you are trying to fatten her up for the winter.

Ingredients:

2 eggs – well beaten
1 cup of sugar
½ cup scalded milk
2 TBSP butter
1 tsp vanilla
1 cup flour
½ tsp salt
1 ½ tsp baking powder

Prep:

In a large mixing bowl beat eggs; add the sugar and beat mixture well. Melt butter in the scalded milk and add to bowl. Mix flour, baking powder and salt and stir into the bowl. Stir in vanilla. Pour mixture into a greased 8" or 9" cake pan and bake at 350 degrees for 20 to 25 minutes.

You can add frosting, fruit, and ice cream or have it plain.

Love all, trust a few. Do wrong to none.
– William Shakespeare –

Boston Cream Pie

DOGHOUSE ALERT:

MODERATE

Caution − 1.) The fattening-her-up-for-the-winter-thing and 2.) If the filling is a little lumpy, do not tell her you were shooting for the consistency of her gravy.

Ingredients:

1 Aunt Mary Dugan's Sponge Cake
¾ cup sugar
½ cup flour
¼ tsp salt
2 cups milk
2 egg yolks slightly beaten
2 TBSP butter
1 tsp vanilla

Prep:

Combine sugar, flour and salt in a saucepan. Stir in the milk and cook over low heat, stirring constantly until thick. Add the egg yolks and continue to cook stirring for 3 minutes. Remove from heat and blend in the butter and vanilla. Let cool for 15 minutes.

Split the sponge cake into two layers and spread the cream filling between layers. Top with a thin layer of chocolate frosting (I do not do frostings, so I buy some ready made, but if you can make a thin chocolate confectioner frosting you will be in heaven).

One word frees us from all the weight and pain of life:
That word is love.
– Sophocles –

Berry Pie

DOGHOUSE ALERT:

MODERATE

The crust recipe is not for the calorie counter and please no stems or leaves.

Ingredients:

BERRY MIXTURE:
  2 cups berries (raspberries or blackberries)
  1 ½ cups sugar
  2 TBSP flour

CRUST:
  2 cups flour
  1 tsp salt
  1 cup Crisco (might want to hide the recipe from her)
  2/3 cups ice water

Prep:

BERRY MIXTURE:
  In a large bowl add berries, sugar and flour and mix well (do not break up the berries)

CRUST:

Mix flour, salt and Crisco but cutting them in together with two forks or pastry cutter. Add ice water and mix until dough can be handled (add a small amount of flour if needed). Divide the dough into halves and roll out crust on a flour-dusted surface. Place in a 9-inch pie pan and fill with your berry mixture. Cover with top crust and cut in several slits as vents. Preheat oven to 425 degrees and place pie in center rack. Lower heat to 400 degrees immediately and bake for 20 minutes. Lower the oven to 375 degrees and continue baking for 20 minutes. Turn oven to 350 degrees and finish baking for 20 minutes. Watch pie, if edges of crust start to brown too much; cover them with foil for the last 20 minutes.

Laughter is the sun that drives
winter from the human face.
– Victor Hugo –

Fruit Parfait Amour

DOGHOUSE ALERT:

LOW

Just be ready for the "Do you think I am fat?" thing. Your pat answer is always, "You? No way!"

Ingredients:

Berry version:

> Strawberries
> Blueberries
> Raspberries
> Flavored yogurt

Prep:

Wash and de-stem all fruit and cut the strawberries into ¼ or ½ inch slices. In a fruit cup or parfait glass add 1-inch layers starting with fruit at the bottom and alternate with 1-inch layers of yogurt and fruit.

Melon version:

> Cantaloupe
> Mango
> Honeydew

Flavored yogurt
Nutmeg

Prep:

Using a melon baller, scoop pieces of fruit and place into a fruit cup or parfait glass in 1-inch layers and alternate layers of yogurt and fruit. Top off with a dusting of nutmeg.

Manners maketh man.
- William of Wykeham -

Jed's Caramel Surprise

DOGHOUSE ALERT:
NOT EVEN WORTH TRYING

This recipe is when you want to go to the dog house and want a sure way to end up there, although probably longer than you want.

Ingredients:

Whipped cream
Caramel syrup

Prep:

Fill bowl with whipped cream (since this is a lazy recipe use store bought ready made whipped cream). Pour caramel syrup over whipped cream making sure you add enough to bring you right to the edge of sickness.

Tell me what you eat, and I will tell you what you are.
– Anthelme Brillat-Savarin –

Printed in the United States
61550LVS00004B/8

9 781598 000252